WORKING WITH WORDS
Adding Life to Your Oral Presentations

RAE A. STONEHOUSE

COPYRIGHT:

Copyright © 2020 by Rae A. Stonehouse
All rights reserved.
No part of this book may be reproduced in any form or by any electronic or mechanical means, including information storage and retrieval systems, without written permission from the author, except for the use of brief quotations in a book review.

Live For Excellence Productions
1221 Velrose Drive
Kelowna, B.C., Canada
V1X6R7
https://liveforexcellence.com

I

CHAPTER ONE: INTRODUCTION

Forrest Gump is known for having said ***Life*** is ***like*** a box of chocolates.

It occurred to me in a dream one night, that life is more like a bowl of strawberries. More precisely, ***public speaking*** is like a bowl of ***strawberries***.

Let me explain.

A few strawberries, freshly picked off the plant and immediately eaten, can be delicious.

A bushel basket of them sitting in front of you with the expectation you had to eat them *here* and *now*, wouldn't be.

But what about a nice strawberry sundae or a good-sized mouth-watering portion of strawberry shortcake?

I'm salivating thinking about either of them, actually both of them...

When it comes to public speaking, there are times when *fewer* words are *better*.

There are times we are bombarded with a speaker telling us *everything* they know about a subject.

There's too much to absorb... so we tune out.

Then there is the ***strawberry shortcake*** of presentations.

This is where the speaker whets your appetite, gives you *just* enough of a serving that you are close to being full and leaves you wanting more.

This book focuses on using words to help you become a dynamic speaker.

Let's get started!

How many words are there in the English language?

According to the Second Edition of the 20-volume Oxford English Dictionary, there are:

- Full entries for 171,476 words in current use
- 47,156 obsolete words
- 9,500 derivative words included as subentries

Words have the power to **poison**, to **hurt**, to **heal** or to **bless**.

You can have a *powerful* delivery, an *expressive* voice, an *attractive* appearance, and *thorough knowledge* of your subject but if your words are *poorly* chosen, your speech will fail to communicate.

With the *right* words, you can *communicate* your thoughts, your *feelings*, and your *emotions*.

And with the *right* words you can *teach* people, give them *understanding*, *entertain* them, **persuade** them to change attitudes, and even *persuade* them to do your bidding.

But before you can do any of that, you should learn as much as possible about words.

❦

DID YOU KNOW THAT YOU HAVE THREE VOCABULARIES? IN THE next chapter, we look at each of them in detail.

❦

"It's okay to send flowers, but don't let the flowers do all the talking. Flowers have a limited vocabulary. About the best flowers can say is that you remembered. But your words tell the rest." Jim Rohn

"Vocabulary enables us to interpret and to express. If you have a limited vocabulary, you will also have a limited vision and a limited future." Jim Rohn

The difference between the right word and the almost right word is the difference between lightning and a lightning bug. Mark Twain (1835-1910)

CHAPTER TWO: YOU HAVE THREE VOCABULARIES

Welcome to **Chapter Two** where we explore the *three vocabularies* each of us has to add life to our oral presentations.

THESE ARE:

1. Your reading vocabulary — Made up of words you *know* when you *see* them in print.

2. Your writing vocabulary — It's *smaller* than your reading vocabulary, for you *wouldn't* use many of the words you recognize in print when you write a letter or report.

3. Your speaking vocabulary — This is the *smallest* of the three because it is *limited* by the listener's *word knowledge* and by your ***ability*** to speak the word so they hear it.

Thus, many of the words you know when you see them in print or use them when you write are of ***little use*** to you in speaking.

Speak only "Speaking" words!

I'm reminded of an old Toastmaster friend of mine... Wally.

Wally was a retired newspaper journalist who had dedicated his working life to creating stories in print, come alive.

When it came to delivering oral presentations, he had some difficulty. He had written his speeches to be read.

When he went to deliver them orally, he found his sentences were too long and wordy and he lost his audience.

When we read a paragraph in a book, we have the punctuation marks serving as road signs if you will.

We can see when we need to stop.

We can tell if a sentence is a question or not based on there being a question mark at the end of the sentence.

We can also reread a sentence or paragraph if we don't grasp its meaning the first time.

Not so with content delivered orally. We only have one chance in listening to what a speaker has to say to us.

We can't go back and re-listen to what they said.

They have already gone on to delivering new content.

As a speaker, that means we have to craft our message clearly, so our audience understands it the first time.

COMPARING AND CONTRASTING ORAL & WRITTEN Communication

There are many differences between communicating in *writing* and communicating in *speech* — one-to-one or one-to-many.

Let's look at some differences between the two.

Because talking is *face-to-face* and *personal*, it is much more *direct* than writing.

Hand and body gestures, facial expressions, and vocal variety help greatly to support face-to-face communication.

It is also reinforced by instant feedback from listeners in the form of smiles, frowns, applause, catcalls, clenched fists, and so on.

An alert speaker who is *sensitive* to feedback can "shift gears" and adapt to changing circumstances.

Writing, however, depends *solely* on words and punctuation to deliver the message.

There are no *gestures* and no *voice*, and if there is any feedback, it takes time to reach the writer.

Good talking is *wordy*, *repetitive*, and *far less structured* than efficient writing.

(Perhaps that's why so many more people find *talking well* easier than *writing well*.)

A good speech, reproduced *word for word* on paper, usually *does not* read well because it rambles and repeats words and thoughts.

It is not nearly as disciplined and organized as good writing.

Effective talking is *aimed* at people's minds and hearts through their ears... and ears prefer short, direct, conversational sentences.

Long involved sentences are acceptable in writing for two reasons:

- The eye can *absorb* many more words in an instant than a speaker can *say*.
- If a reader stumbles on a marathon sentence, they can reread it at their leisure.

Not so with spoken words — once uttered they're gone, especially in a speech.

If a listener misses a sentence, both she and the speaker have lost part of the message; there is no going back, except perhaps during the question-and-answer period.

In a conversation, of course, the listener can ask the speaker to repeat.

IN THE NEXT CHAPTER, WE LOOK AT THE **LANGUAGE** OF speaking.

Well chosen words mixed with measured emotions is the basis of affecting people." Jim Rohn

"The two great words of antiquity are **behold** and **beware**. Behold the possibilities and beware the temptations." Jim Rohn

"What is written without effort is in generally read without pleasure." Samuel Johnson (1709-1784)

CHAPTER THREE: THE LANGUAGE OF SPEAKING

Welcome to **Chapter Three** where we look at the *language of speaking* to add life to your oral presentations.

USE SHORT, SIMPLE SENTENCES WITH ACTION VERBS AND ONE idea per sentence. 5-20 words per sentence.

- Use contractions, sentence fragments, short words, slang.
- Use personal stories, experiences.
- Employ concrete, specific picture producing words.
- Use personal pronouns I, me, we, us, you, they.
- Receive immediate feedback.
- Repeat your message, saying it different ways.
- Avoid the passive voice. The active voice relies on verbs.
- Avoid modifiers. Example: "I think that maybe,""perhaps,""you know."

- Reinforce words with facial expression, voice, gestures and movement.
- Eliminate distracting vocalized pauses i.e. ums, ers, ahs.
- Add pauses and silence for dramatic effect or emphasis.
- Use words that your audience will understand.

Let's look at using **shared meanings**.

A trouble spot for speakers comes from using words the audience *does not* understand.

At the onset, you should understand there is nothing particularly wrong with using terms the audience doesn't understand — *as long* as you explain the terms in language they *can* understand.

Another way of stating this principal is that you should explain your terms in the *audience's* language.

You can make your speeches more effective by learning various methods of communicating *meaning* to an audience.

The following eight methods are a sampling of ways to *evoke* the meanings you intend.

We'll list them here then expand upon each of them in a moment.

Types of Definitions:

- Comparison
- Contrasts
- Synonyms
- Antonyms
- Etymology
- Differentiation
- Operational definition
- Experiential definition

Let's start off with Comparisons.

Comparisons:

Something *unfamiliar* can be defined by showing how it is *similar* to something the audience is more familiar with.

Public speakers should be careful to avoid comparisons that have been *overused*, such as "smooth as silk", "pretty as a picture", or "hard as a rock."

These overused similes or comparisons are called *cliches*.

Instead, try to make comparisons that helps the audience envision what the speaker describes.

Example: describing snow as "a soft, rolling white carpet."

Contrasts:

Something *similar* can be defined by showing how it is *different* from something else the audience is more familiar with.

Synonyms:

To define a term with *synonyms* is to use words *close* to or *similar* in meaning and more *familiar* to the audience.

"Being spaced out," said a speaker who was defining the term, "is similar, to having your mind go blank, being dumbfounded, or being disoriented."

Antonyms:

To define a term with *antonyms* is to use words that are *opposite* in meaning and that are more *familiar* to the audience.

Hence, being "spaced out," is "not being alert, keen, or responsive."

Etymology:

To define a term by means of its *etymology* is to give its *origins* or *history*.

A desk dictionary will reveal the language or languages from which a word is derived.

More specialized sources like the Dictionary of Mythology, the Oxford English Dictionary, and the Etymological Dictionary of Modern English will provide more detailed accounts.

In a speech of *definition*, a speaker used the etymology of a word to explain its significance:

Example: What does rhinoplasty mean?

Well, without a dictionary, you might feel you're lost.

But if you break up the word into its two parts, **rhino** and **plasty**, the meaning becomes clearer.

You might not know the meaning of rhino itself, but if you think of an animal whose name bears this prefix, namely the rhinoceros, and of the most distinctive feature of this beast, its rather large snout, you would probably guess correctly that 'rhino' refers to the nose.

The meaning of the suffix 'plasty' also seems elusive, but a more common form of it, plastic, reveals its meaning of "molding or formation."

Put together, these meanings have been modified to create the current medical definition of **rhinoplasty** "a plastic surgical operation on the nose, either reconstructive, restorative, or cosmetic."

Put quite simply, a *rhinoplasty* is a nose job.

Differentiation:

To define a term by means of *differentiation* is to *distinguish* it from other members of the same class.

For Example:

Some people think a jury trial is a jury trial; they don't realize a jury trial can be quite different, depending on whether the case being tried is a *civil* or a *criminal* case.

If it is a *criminal* case, then the jury will have to decide guilt or innocence beyond a reasonable doubt; if the trial is a *civil* case, then the preponderance of evidence should decide whether the plaintiff or the defendant wins the case.

The end result of a jury trial in a criminal case is guilt or innocence, with the former resulting in punishment.

The end result of a jury trial in a civil case is damages, either granted or not.

Operational Definition:

An *operational definition* reveals the meaning of a term by *describing how* it is made or what it does.

A cake can be operationally defined by the recipe, the operations that must be performed to make it.

A job classification, such as secretary, can be operationally defined by the tasks the person in that job is expected to perform: a secretary is a person who takes dictation, types, and files papers.

Here is an *operational definition* from a student speech:

"Modern rhinoplasty is done for both cosmetic and health reasons. It consists of several mini-operations.

First, if the septum separating the nostrils has become deviated as a result of an injury or some other means, it is straightened with surgical pliers.

Then, if the nose is to be remodelled, small incisions are made within each nostril, and working entirely within the nose, the surgeon is able to remove, reshape, or redistribute the bone and cartilage lying underneath the skin.

Finally, if the nose is crooked, a chisel is taken to the bones of the upper nose, and they are broken so that they may be straightened and centered."

Experiential Definition:

A term can be explained by revealing a person's *experience* with it.

Often words are ones used only by a specific group who have shared experiences.

The kids at a local high school call the rural kids "reds."

In some circles calling someone a "red" might mean they are a communist, but in this case the high schoolers mean the "reds" are "rednecks," a slang expression for country folks.

Another example of a term that can only be understood through experiential definition are the "posties" on campus.

The "posties" are students who have served as writers and editors of the university's daily newspaper, The Post.

Perhaps you too can think of terms that are used by a gang, an organization, or an ethnic group that can be explained only by revealing those people's experience with the word.

WORKING WITH WORDS

In our next chapter, we look at words that are worth *forgetting*, meaning you should remove them from your vocabulary.

❧

"The purpose of speaking is to order, clarify and intensify the experience for the audience." Patricia Fripp

"Remember not only to say the right thing in the right place, but far more difficult still, to leave unsaid the wrong thing at the tempting moment." Benjamin Franklin

"There are two types of speakers; those that are nervous and those that are liars." Mark Twain

CHAPTER FOUR: WORDS WORTH FORGETTING

Welcome to **Chapter Four** where we explore *words worth forgetting* to add life to your oral presentations.

THERE ARE SOME TYPES OR CLASSIFICATIONS OF WORDS WE should remove from our speaking vocabulary to help with our understandability.

 1. Words people might not understand: Substitute "good times" for "halcyon", "pleasure-seeker" for "hedonist"

 2. Words of doubtful meaning: Examples: ameliorate, abstruse, maudlin

 3. Words you can't pronounce: Ameliorate from the last item might be an example. It's a bit of a tongue-twister.

 4. Made-up words: When my son was six years old he coined the term 'skuggy' to describe chewing gum that had lost its flavour. *Skuggy* is a made-up word.

 5. Words of many meanings: A Frenchman said this about learning the English language: "I discovered that if I was *quick* I was fast, if I *spent* too freely I was fast, if I *cut down* on food it was a fast, if a woman hung out in bars she was fast. I was discouraged!"

5. Words difficult to hear: Individuals with hearing loss can have difficulty hearing and understanding certain words or parts of words. When speaking, your voice may be audible, but separate words may sound mixed up or blurred together. Rhyming or words that are similar such as cat/cap, bread/thread, pool/cool, are extremely difficult to distinguish when the listener has a hearing loss.

6. Word combinations that confuse: Alliterations can add to your presentation, but they may be confusing for some individuals. An alliteration is defined as 'the occurrence of the same letter or sound at the beginning of adjacent or closely connected words.' A classic example is: "She sells seashells by the sea-shore."

7. Loaded words: Some words that concern race, religion, politics, and personal character can provoke heated and sometimes overpowering reactions. Loaded words can induce people to commit irrational acts. Loaded words are like a loaded gun; they can cause devastating damage.

8. Cliches: Cliches are expressions that have been kicked around so often they are now shopworn, threadbare, and meaningless. Since they reflect a sparse vocabulary and a pallid imagination, avoid them at all costs. I've often heard it said that you should avoid clichés... like the plague.

A self-fulfilling cliché... I wonder?

10. Euphemisms: Euphemisms are silly inoffensive little words or phrases used as substitutes for stronger, perhaps harmful ones. Saying that someone is going #1 or #2 instead of urinating or defecating is a common example.

Then there is the military use of the euphemism *'collateral damage.'* That's their way of saying that innocent citizens were killed.

I𝑛 the next chapter we explore how to improve *your descriptive powers* to add life to your oral presentations.

"It is better to keep your mouth closed and let people think you are a fool than to open it and remove all doubt." Mark Twain (1835-1910)

"Words are not only evil in themselves; but they infect the soul with evil." Socrates (470-399 B.C.)

"Get your facts first and then you can distort them as much as you please." Mark Twain

CHAPTER FIVE: IMPROVING YOUR DESCRIPTIVE POWERS

Welcome to Chapter Five where we explore how to improve ***your descriptive powers*** to add life to your oral presentations.

※

HOW CAN YOU IMPROVE YOUR LANGUAGE IN PUBLIC SPEAKING?

Public speakers need to have a large vocabulary and good descriptive powers in order to accurately and vividly convey their thoughts.

The person who only knows the primary colors of blue, red and yellow — is unable to describe a landscape as the person who knows how to *differentiate* mauve, chartreuse, indigo, violet and purple.

A person's descriptions typically relate size, shape, color, texture, or even feelings evoked by objects and people.

One method of describing something is to use precise, accurate language. Here is an example of precise and accurate language.

Two individuals proceeded towards the apex of a natural geologic protuberance, the purpose of their expedition being the procurement of a sample of fluid hydride of oxygen in a large vessel, the exact size of which was unspecified.

One member of the team precipitously descended, sustaining severe damage to the upper cranial portion of his anatomical structure; subsequently the second member of the team performed a self-rotational translation oriented in the same direction taken by the first team member.

In everyday language...

Jack and Jill went up the hill to fetch a pail of water. Jack fell down and broke his crown and Jill came tumbling after!

Even though it is technically correct, you need to speak using words that your audience will understand. Speaking means using shorter words, shorter sentences. Your audience shouldn't have to pull out their dictionary or thesaurus to understand your speech.

Build Your Vocabulary: A second method of describing something is to use a variety of words and expressions.

A basketball's surface texture is described as "coarseness," "typography," and "an undulating surface infiltrated by scores of bulging protuberances."

The snow is "soft," "rolling," and "white."

The "serene earth," in the stalling maneuver becomes "spinning fields," as the engine makes a "lugging sound," and "labors into a steeper and steeper climb."

The vocabulary in each case is impressive in its variety and appropriateness.

It's not how many words you know. The more words you know the better but no matter how many you know, your success depends on *how* you use the words you know.

You can't use all the words you know in speaking.

Every word you know today is not a good speaking word.

Employ Denotative and Connotative Meanings: A third method of describing something is to use the *connotative dimension* of words.

A **Denotative** meaning is the dictionary meaning, the *objective* meaning without an *emotional* component.

A **Connotative** meaning is what the word suggests, its *emotional* content.

For instance, if you refer to a woman as a "broad," the *denotative* definition may mean a *female*, but the connotative definition probably means a sex object.

The same thing holds for a man referred to as a "hunk."

State the Familiar in an Unfamiliar Way: A fourth method of describing something is to state the familiar in an unfamiliar way to make it more striking and memorable.

"The bird carried the sky on its wings," is more exciting imagery than "the bird flew across the sky."

To make your speeches more effective, use precise, accurate language; employ a wide vocabulary; use both the denotative and connotative meaning of words; make comparisons; and state the familiar in an unfamiliar way.

Learn new words by reading self-help books, stories, and poems; by listening carefully to how literate people use the language.

Use resources like the dictionary, the thesaurus, and handbooks on grammar and usage.

Learning how to express yourself through language is not an easy task, though people who do it well make it look easy.

Provide Clarity: If the audience *doesn't* understand the message instantly, then the speaker has, to some extent, *failed*.

Thus, *every* possible measure must be taken to ensure all her words and thoughts are perfectly clear to the audience.

Throughout your talk, words are your prime means for helping your audience understand your message.

Devices that will help you achieve clarity in your talk are *summaries* and *transition*s.

If your talk consists of three well-researched major points, list those three points in your introduction so your audience will know at once what ground you will cover.

Discuss them in depth, summarize them at the end of your talk, and emphasize any conclusions that they lead to.

Another aid to clarity is the use of *transitions* — words that indicate the connections between ideas — which show whether you are continuing in the same vein or are about to shift to another topic.

Confucius, the Chinese philosopher, said it all 2400 years ago: "In language clearness is everything."

Ensure Accuracy: As a conscientious speaker, your information should be as current and as accurate as research can make it.

The surest and quickest way for you to damage your credibility is to spew forth misinformation.

Use appropriate language: In addition to being *precise,* the language should also be suitable to the subject, audience and occasion.

The use of slang depends largely on the occasion of your talk and on the relationship between you and the audience.

At a formal or even semi-formal affair, slang would violate good taste even if you know almost all the guests.

In any case, it's important to resist the temptation to overuse slang; too much will degrade any talk.

Don't overkill with too much information: It is relatively easy for a knowledgeable speaker to provide more information than an audience without expertise in that particular area can easily absorb.

I hope I'm not doing it right now with all the information I am providing you on this subject.

In our next chapter we talk about talking. We've crafted and finely tuned our message, now how do we make it come alive?

"When you speak, your talk must be emotionally and intellectually satisfying." Patricia Fripp

First learn the meaning of what you say, and then speak. Epictetus (55-135)

"When I use a word," Humpty Dumpty said in rather a scornful tone, "it means just what I choose it to mean - neither more nor less." Lewis Carroll (1832-1898)

CHAPTER SIX: USING VOCAL VARIETY TO MAKE YOUR PRESENTATION COME ALIVE

Welcome to **Chapter Six** where we explore how to use *vocal variety* to add life to your oral presentations.

TO MAKE YOUR SPEECH EFFECTIVE AND INTERESTING, CERTAIN techniques can be applied.

Vocal variety is the way we use our voice to create interest, excitement and emotional involvement.

However, it is important not to sound false or as if you are giving a performance.

Whilst words convey meaning, how they are said reflects feelings and emotions.

A good voice is:
a. **Articulate** — meaning that it is clear and distinct
b. **Expressive** — it portrays different *shades* of meaning
c. **Vital** — it is alive and enthusiastic
d. **Pleasing** — the tone is pleasant to the ear
e. **Relaxed** — it is free from tension and affectation

Affectation meaning behavior, speech, or writing that is artificial and designed to impress. I had to look it up!

f. And finally, a good voice is: **Personalized** — In that it is appropriate to the age, gender and image you desire.

IN THE NEXT CHAPTER, WE LOOK AT FOUR VOICE VARIABLES: **pitch, rate, volume and quality**.

"Say all you have to say in the fewest possible words, or your reader will be sure to skip them; and in the plainest possible words or he will certainly misunderstand them." John Ruskin (1819 - 1900)

"Make everything as simple as possible but not simpler." Albert Einstein

"Words do two major things: They provide food for the mind and create light for understanding and awareness." Jim Rohn

CHAPTER SEVEN: USING VOICE VARIABLES

Welcome to **Chapter Seven** where we explore using *voice variables* to add life to your oral presentations.

———

EACH OF THE FOLLOWING VARIABLES ARE USED IN VARYING degrees to add interest to your voice and speech.

We take a closer look at each of these variables over the next few chapters.

Clarity: Let's start off with your voice *clarity*.

Some people tend to speak through clenched teeth and with little movement of their lips. It is this inability to open mouths and failure to make speech sounds with precision that is the root cause of inaudibility.

The sound is locked into the mouth and not let out.

To have good articulation it is important to unclench the jaw open the mouth and give full benefit to each sound you make, paying particular attention to the ends of words.

This will also help your audience as a certain amount of lip-reading will be possible.

When speaking in public, try to convey the information with as much vocal energy and enthusiasm as possible.

This does not mean your voice has to swoop and dive all over the place uncontrolled. Try to make the talk interesting and remember that when you are nervous or even excited, vocal chords tense and shorten causing the voice to get higher.

Emphasize certain words and phrases within the talk to convey their importance and help to add variety.

Pitch refers to the lowness and the highness of the tone or sound in your voice.

The best pitch range is at least 8 notes. A narrow range, bores listeners and they'll quickly "tune out."

We have all heard speakers that we would describe as being monotone. That is, their voice never changes. We get tired of them and we stop listening to them.

A good speaker may use as many as 25 different notes to convey variety and meaning. This is more often a problem for men than for women, because men sometimes (consciously or unconsciously) try not to express too much emotion and, as a result, can sound "flat."

Although women generally use more pitch variety, they sometimes get into an upper pitch range, stay there too long and can sound "shrill."

Let's look at some pitch variables.

The pitch is too high.

Under normal circumstances, this frequently occurs because of nervousness (remember your first talk?), fright or from being overanxious to respond.

If you suffer no physical problems that may affect your voice, the more often you speak, the more relaxed your throat muscles will become, resulting in more pleasant vocal sounds.

I experienced this problem myself when I first started to develop my public speaking skills. At the time, I didn't know how to express my enthusiasm when I spoke.

I tended to speak an octave or two higher than I normally

speak. My wife said I sounded like Donald Duck delivering a speech.

It took me a while to become confident enough in my speaking that I was able to comfortably speak within my normal range.

The pitch is too low.

You may know some people who speak with a very low, bass-like sound.

Usually they speak slowly.

Reading aloud happy, lively material — children's books for example — at a fast pace is a good exercise that may help to raise a low pitch.

Monotone:

To avoid or eliminate a monotone, you must find your normal range. Just in case the term monotone isn't clear to you, it is where a person speaks in one tone.

There are no ups and downs. Every word comes out sounding the same.

It can be difficult to determine where one sentence or thought ends, and a new one begins.

Normal?

This is the vocal area that is most comfortable for you to carry on a normal conversation and from which you may easily raise or lower your pitch.

Everybody's normal, is likely different.

Once you establish your normal pitch range, it is crucial to maintain it.

Listen to how it sounds and feels when you use it so that whenever you speak, it becomes as natural as breathing.

Inflections:

Inflections comprise another important characteristic of speech.

An *inflection* is a raised pitch — a high note used to add emphasis to a word. The up-and-down inflection of your pitch adds color to your delivery.

A single change in inflection may often change the meaning or implication of a sentence.

"How dare you use that tone of voice on me!"

Let's take a look at an example of inflection in action in the simple sentence of "I said he was no good."

The inflection is on *different* words in the same sentence.

Try reading each sentence out loud to get a sense of how inflection can change the meaning of what you are saying.

Example:

<u>I</u> said he was no good.

I **said** he was no good

I said **he** was no good

I said he **was** no good

I said he was **no** good

I said he was no **good**.

I think you will agree with me that while it is the exact same sentence, the inflection changes the meaning of the sentence.

Do you use HRTs?

I have to admit, the term HRT was new to me until I discovered it my research for this book. I was aware of the habit, not necessarily there was a term for the habit.

HRT stands for *high-rise terminals...* which really doesn't explain it at all, does it?

It is the habit of some speakers to raise the inflection of the *final* word in each sentence so it comes across sounding like a question.

Some call it up talk. We mainly hear it in young people.

When used frequently, it appears that the speaker is asking a lot of questions, when really, they are making statements.

It leaves the listener confused as to the real meaning of what is being expressed.

A lilt at the end of a spoken sentence may also leave the impression in the listener that the speaker is unsure of themselves.

They sound hesitant in their sentence, like they are putting the words out there, but they are not sure if they are right or wrong, whether they actually believe in what they are saying, or they are being defensive and preparing to defend what they said if the listener disagrees.

Vocal Exercises:

Here are some vocal exercises to help improve your vocal pitch. Some sage advice is to always work gently when you do voice exercises.

Your voice may get tired as do other muscles when you use them, but it should never HURT.

1. Start on a comfortably low tone and count up the scale as high as you can without straining.

Then count back down.

Don't "gravel" at the bottom.

2. Starting at your normal pitch, say "I have a good voice."

Repeat three times, getting higher each time.

Go back to normal and go lower three times.

※

IN THE NEXT CHAPTER, WE EXPLORE YOUR *SPEAKING RATE*.

※

Speak properly, and in as few words as you can, but always plainly; for the end of speech is not ostentation, but to be understood. William Penn (1644-1718)

"Better understated than overstated. Let people be surprised that it was more than you promised and easier than you said." Jim Rohn

It's not the matter you cover so much as it is the manner in which you cover it." Jim Rohn

CHAPTER EIGHT: YOUR SPEAKING RATE

In this chapter we continue exploring voice variables, focusing on your ***speaking rate*** to add life to your oral presentations.

RATE:

For almost everyone, a comfortable speaking rate lies between 130 and 160 words per minute.

Speaking too fast can cause poor diction — running words together, slurring words, and dropping word endings — which could result in listeners complaining "What did he say?"

Speaking too quickly is a bad habit and it can be difficult for people to keep up with you or even understand what you're saying.

This makes it easy for them to tune out and stop listening.

When I was a beginning student of public speaking my speech evaluators, described my speaking as being staccato.

I wasn't aware of its meaning until I looked it up.

Staccato speech is where you speak in fragments of sentences that are punctuated by pauses, which interrupt, to the point of destroying the flow of your speech.

Such speech is abrupt, broken, and usually quite hard to follow for long periods of time, and may make the speaker look confused or focused on something.

A machine-gun delivery like this can easily lose your listeners.

When I self-reflected on why I was delivering my speeches this way, I determined the cause was the way I memorized my speeches.

I would memorize the speech in chunks, or paragraphs. I would memorize the content, word for word.

When I was delivering my speech, each piece would come into my memory as a chunk. I would deliver the chunk, then move onto the next chunk of the speech.

To resolve this habit, I learned a different way to memorize my speech.

My new way may seem somewhat counter intuitive. To memorize the content, I don't memorize the content.

I create my presentations so they are like a road map. I start off with an introduction to get the speech going, then I move into the first stop on the trip.

Each topic or variance on the story becomes a chunk, or a story in its own right. I practice each chunk of my story, so I know it inside out.

It isn't memorized word for word. What happens is I am prepared to deliver a chunk in multiple ways should I need to adapt it.

I do memorize the order of the story in chunks, like following the towns and cities on a road map so that I can easily follow my overall speech, going from one story to another.

Your *rate* should be appropriate for your material.

As you would expect, serious content is going to be paced more slowly than that which is light and upbeat.

Be careful not to let yourself get too fast or you'll stumble and get sloppy. You'll also risk 'wearing out' your audience.

On the other hand... talking too slowly is just as bad.

Actually, it can irritate your listeners even more than talking too fast.

When a speaker takes, like what seems five minutes to draaaaag out a phrase or sentence, they are setting up their listeners to yawn or mind-wander.

A sluggish speaker can easily convey an impression of shyness, lack of confidence or intelligence, or illness.

Speech rate is simply the speed at which you speak. It's calculated in the number of words spoken in a minute (wpm.)

Good Pacing:

Good pacing means having an interesting rate of delivery, with enough variation to hold your listener's interest.

While in your head you might think your pace is perfect, in reality, you might be off the mark.

This is where finding out your speech rates can be helpful. To describe excitement, you would speed up your delivery. And maybe your pitch as well, as we mentioned in an earlier section.

When quoting statistics or emphasizing several points, you would slow down your pace. This gives your listeners a chance to process the information you have just given them.

Speaking at a constant rate, either fast or slow, can only lead to monotony and loss of your audience.

If you're a "rusher," practice your material very, very slowly. It should feel painfully slow.

When you get in front of the audience, you'll probably speed up again, but not to your previous rate.

Practice reading stories at an obviously "wrong" pace.

Read an obituary very quickly, read the results of the 4-H fair very slowly, etc. Then go back and read them at an appropriate rate.

This exercise will sensitize you to feeling what is most "*right*."

The Power of Pausing: Make Use of the Dramatic Pause

Pausing is one of the most powerful weapons in your arsenal of speaking techniques, because... this unspoken word can take a well written speech and make it come alive for your audience... if done correctly.

A pause is an unspoken word.

Pauses keep listeners in suspense and add variety, excitement and interest to your delivery.

We pause for one of four reasons:

- to provide emphasis
- to breathe
- to provide variety in delivery
- to pull your thoughts together

For example, let's say you have been devoting yourself in finding ways to clean up the environment, and you want to share that information with other people.

So you write your speech and in it you include many powerful statements.

The speech is delivered, however you did not receive the enthusiastic response you were hoping for.

What was missing from the delivery of your speech?

What the audience may not have seen were the visible and auditory clues that your presence on the stage did not convey.

Your whole demeanor... your whole body has to show your enthusiasm... before your audience can see that you are truly passionate about your topic.

The passionate statements you deliver demand... a long pause at the end of each sentence... combined with purposeful eye contact as you scan the audience.

This will solidify your connection with your audience because, it all comes down to being credible and authentic towards your audience.

It is not enough to simply stand there... and regurgitate words.

When you are presenting impactful statements to your audience that may be shocking in content, *or* you are telling them something they knew nothing about, and are impressed with your knowledge on this subject, *you will want to make sure you are getting your message across.*

Now, I am going to demonstrate why a well written speech, with all its powerful statements, can be far more effective when we use the technique of... pausing.

Pausing and eye contact work in unison to make that vital connection with your audience.

I will now give you an example of an impactful statement using pauses and then I will repeat the same example without pauses and then compare the two.

Obviously, I won't be able to demonstrate the eye contact part of the example.

"If we as a society don't do something soon to stop the threat of global warming... Polar Bears... could become extinct... we need to act quickly to prevent that from happening."

The reason we need to pause after an impactful statement is to show respect for our audience by allowing them to absorb the impact of what you just said before you carry on, at the same time making eye contact with your audience.

This is an acknowledgment between the speaker and the audience which forms a bond.

You are showing through this technique that you truly believe and care about what you are telling your audience and can instantly make that connection, even if they don't realize it is happening.

When eye contact is made, each person can feel as though the speaker is talking only to them, which again cement's that bond.

You as the speaker will need to help the audience feel the impact of that statement the same way you felt it the first time you heard it or read it.

Therefore, you have to bring yourself back to a time in

history when you first became passionate about the topic and let the audience feel that passion as well.

Now, I will repeat that earlier sentence without pausing.

"If we as a society don't do something soon to stop the threat of global warming Polar Bears could become extinct, so we need to act quickly to prevent that from happening."

With no emphasis on the content, I can't convince you to see the importance of what I just said, and you may not trust my sincerity on this subject.

You run the risk of losing your audience.

The audience may be left thinking that you weren't authentic with the statement because your physical delivery did not show that you put enough emphasis on the impactful statement you just delivered.

The sentence is impactful, but it was not reflected that way to the audience. So, the speaker loses out on making that important connection.

What you risk by not putting emphasis on an impactful statement, and not pausing long enough for the audience to absorb what you just said is, losing the audience's attention immediately after the statement.

The audience may start thinking to themselves, "What, I didn't know Polar Bears were at risk".

Now they are deep in thought and are not listening to your next comments.

That's why it is very important to give the appropriate time to pause, allow them to absorb what you said, and then carry on. Then whatever you say after will hopefully keep the audience's attention.

When you are writing your speech, you need to look at where pauses will need to be inserted.

As well, add them as you practice when the speech is completed.

What if you are speaking at the lectern with notes and you are presenting a speech with impactful statements?

How would you handle it?

It can be done but you may not be able to make the connection because of the barrier between you and the audience.

Again, it comes down to how to integrate your notes with eye contact and using pauses.

If you look down at your notes a lot, you are not making eye contact with your audience.

If you deliver an impactful statement and then end it by looking down at your notes, then you have lost the connection.

If you need to use notes, you will have to practice with that in mind and ensure you do use pauses and eye contact at the appropriate times.

Then there is the speaker who delivers a speech with an effective but *unintended* pause.

A newly elected US senator was giving his maiden speech, when he got to a point in his speech when he said: "Consider Mr. Chairman...", then his mind when blank as he paused with his arm outstretched.

After, people came up to him and said that was a very powerful part of his speech.

Remember this, people who have listened to someone deliver a speech won't always remember who the speaker was or what he or she looked like. But they often remember the message the speaker was trying to convey, even years later.

That is very powerful.

The next time you sit down to write a speech, I want you to remember the phrase "The power of pausing" Because the words you don't utter... may be more important than the words you do.

Final Thoughts for Using Effective Pausing in a Speech:

- A speech is not only the words you say, but how you say them.
- An excellent speech on paper has minimal effect with a rushed delivery.

- Pausing is important in all speeches as it can add drama and suspense.
- A pause can emphasize your message.
- Always pause after an impactful statement.
- You risk losing the audience's attention if no pause is used immediately after an impactful statement.
- When writing a speech, type in the word "pause" at the end of a sentence for practicing purposes.
- Avoiding ahs and ums at the end of a sentence makes room for a pause.
- Use purposeful eye contact when pausing.
- Using notes may create a barrier between you and the audience.
- Find or listen to speakers on YouTube or TV and see if you find their pauses effective.
- A speech is considered successful if you are able to connect with your audience.
- You want your audience to leave remembering what you said.

IN THE NEXT CHAPTER WE FOCUS ON YOUR **SPEAKING VOLUME.**

"Speak softly. If you really want to be heard, lower your voice." Terri Levine

"The future belongs to charismatic communicators who are technically competent." Patricia Fripp

"The first 30 seconds and the last 30 seconds have the most impact in a presentation." Patricia Fripp

CHAPTER NINE: YOUR SPEAKING VOLUME

In this chapter we add life to your oral presentations by focusing on your **speaking volume**.

VOLUME:

This isn't a matter of treating the voice like the volume control on the TV remote.

Some people have naturally soft voices and physically cannot bellow.

Additionally, if the voice is raised too much, tonal quality is lost.

Instead of raising the voice it should be '*projected out*'.

Support the voice with lots of breath - the further you want to project the voice out, the more breath you need.

When talking to a group or meeting, it is important to never aim your talk to the front row or just to the people nearest you, but to consciously project what you have to say to those furthest away.

By developing a *strong voice*, as opposed to a *loud* voice, you will be seen as someone positive.

If you tend to whisper, mumble or speak with your head down, it is much easier for people to talk over you or ignore you.

If you speak too *loudly* or *softly*, your audience will communicate this message to you nonverbally.

For example, when you start to speak, do they all move back in their chairs as if blown there by a gust of wind?

Or do they move up to the edge of their seats, turning their ears in your direction?

The size of the room and audience should determine the volume of your voice.

If you have a soft voice, start by asking the audience, "Can you hear me in back?"

Speaking too loudly or too softly is not only annoying, but it also leads to a breakdown in speaker-listener communication.

Adjust your volume for the situation and make sure you aren't relying on the microphone for the energy that should come from your voice.

Speaking too loudly in normal, everyday conversation is unnecessary and can give the wrong impression.

It's easy to get too "laid-back" when you're seated, so even your practice sessions should be done standing.

If you will be giving a speech to a larger audience, try to rehearse with the amplification system.

Listeners don't want to be shouted at, but they get irritated when they can't hear easily.

A strong, resonant *quality* is ideal, but sometimes you'll need another sound.

Use a variety of vocal qualities to make the characters in your stories distinct from one another and the narrator.

The same is true for broadcasters who record promos or commercials.

It's important to vary your delivery so that they don't all sound the same. Versatility is key.

. . .

PRACTICE EXERCISES:

Try saying *yes* or *no* in as many ways as you can.

Be creative and don't be afraid to be a bit "silly."

Vary your rate, pitch, volume and quality.

For vocal variety practice try reading children's books aloud. Your voice will naturally animate with the story.

Record your voice and listen to it resonate in your head for higher vocal tones, in your throat for the mid-range and deep in your chest for lower vocal tones.

Using more gestures will also help to naturally animate your voice.

We'll explore using gestures in the next lesson.

Make a list of emotions and attitudes, then say yes or no to express them.

Try some other words as well.

Read a news article as different character types: executive, child, sex symbol, snob, etc. Notice how the voice changes.

Add some of the new qualities to your speech and/or broadcast.

It's important to have a balanced, conversational delivery style.

MAINTAIN VOCAL ENERGY: THIS DOESN'T MEAN YOU HAVE TO SHOUT, but it does mean you must keep your energy going all the time.

Put excess energy into your voice by pitching up, avoiding husky tones and using vocal variety.

Release physical tension by engaging your body and using gestures.

Commanding the Audience: Let's now look at commanding your audience. This doesn't mean you're barking orders like a Sargent Major might. It's more like owning or having your audience resonate with you.

You can command your audience by using silence.

USING SILENCE:

While speaking at a level your audience is easily able to hear, there is also power in dramatizing your speech with silence.

Silence is a potent and powerful tool for adding impact and drama to a speech. All speech types can benefit from the use of silence whether they be an impromptu speech or a prepared speech.

A speaker has many tools to capture an audience's attention.

Using silence is one of the most effective as it can be used right from the beginning of the speech. A speaker doesn't have to begin immediately when they reach the podium.

There is often a strong temptation to do so.

Speakers can get caught in the emotion and enthusiasm if they are about to deliver and begin speaking immediately. This premature beginning can lose the impact of the start and the speech!

Capturing an audience's attention from the moment a speaker gets to the podium is often left to the words a speaker uses. However, more impact can be made by the speaker saying nothing at all.

Using silence at the *beginning* of your speech generates:

- Drama
- Impact
- Interest
- Intrigue
- Anticipation

These are all crucial ingredients in getting '*command*' of the audience and making them receptive to what is to follow.

The opening silence can also be used to calm and quieten an audience before the speaker begins their delivery.

The speaker benefits as they have the additional time to think about their delivery before launching into it.

Often, once an audience is receptive, the speaker can begin with either a soft, low-volume delivery or alternatively with a very loud delivery.

Both can make a stronger impact on the audience if they follow an initial silent period.

The duration of the silence needs to be judged by the speaker. It can be from a few seconds in length to a much longer period.

Using Silence During the Speech:

Silence can also be used effectively *during* a speech to gain the advantages mentioned a moment ago.

- Drama
- Impact
- Interest
- Intrigue
- Anticipation

Additionally, it can give the audience a chance to reflect on what has just been said and to 'digest' the content of the message.

Many speakers do not allow for this reflection and carry on with their delivery. Often the points made by them are then missed by the audience.

Using Silence at your Speech Conclusion:

Allowing the audience to 'savor' a speech after the speaker has concluded is helped by the speaker remaining at the podium, in silence.

This gives the audience a chance to react to what they have

heard and also to recognize the speech and the speaker, with applause.

The speaker remains in control during this time. The speaker is then free to judge when it is appropriate to acknowledge the applause and leave the podium.

***

In the next chapter, we focus on the *QUALITY* of your oral presentation.

***

First learn the meaning of what you say, and then speak. Epictetus (55-135)

"Outside of the privacy of your own home, all speaking is 'public speaking'. There is no such thing as 'private speaking'." Patricia Fripp

"What you do speaks so loud that I cannot hear what you say." Ralph Waldo Emerson.

CHAPTER TEN: YOUR SPEAKING QUALITY

In this chapter we add life to your oral presentations by focusing on the *quality* of your speaking.

WE'VE ALL PROBABLY HEARD PRESENTERS OR PERHAPS PEOPLE being interviewed on the radio or TV who interject numerous ums, errs and ahs when they speak.

They can be very painful to listen to.

In Toastmasters, many clubs have a member assigned weekly as an Ah Counter.

Their role is to count the ahs and ums their fellow members utter.

After taking on the role a few times, you can't help but count each one, when you are listening to a speaker.

ELIMINATING VERBAL FILLERS: AVOID USING FILLER WORDS such as ah, um, err that I mentioned before. You may also hear "that is to say", "however", "therefore", etc. as a means of covering silences.

Some people call them *word whiskers*.

Word whiskers are a short phrase used as a *verbal crutch* when speaking.

They allow the speaker to pause to consider their next words, without breaking their flow of delivery.

LET'S LOOK AT ENUNCIATION. SPEAKING CLEARLY IS possibly the most important aspect of developing a good speaking voice. You need to pay close attention to *each and every* word you say... pronouncing it fully and correctly.

Make sure to *open your mouth*, loosen your lips and keep your tongue and teeth in the correct position as you speak.

This may also help eliminate or disguise a lisp, if you have one.

It might feel odd at first, but if you consistently make the effort to pronounce your words correctly, it will soon come naturally to you.

Some will argue that *effective speaking* has nothing to do with the outdated concept of 'elocution' where everyone was encouraged to speak in the same *'correct'* manner.

Rather, effective speaking concerns being able to speak in a public context with confidence and clarity, whilst at the same time reflecting your own personality.

Let's now look at the Effect of Breath on Voice and Speech.

The voice is responsive to emotions and sometimes gets 'blocked', which can prevent or hinder the expression of a range of feelings.

The majority of people breathe *too quickly and shallowly* when they speak, which results in a more *unnatural, nasal* tone.

However, it is possible to use physical exercise to help produce a more flexible voice, in the same way that people who use vocal sounds professionally take lessons, to ensure that their voices are kept in a versatile condition and ready to vocalize a range of sounds.

When under stress, an individual's breathing pattern will change.

When your muscles are tense, you can't use your lungs to their full capacity.

When a person is frightened or nervous, a common symptom is *tension* in the neck and shoulders. This occurs because, when under pressure, *over-breathing* tends to occur.

Plenty of air is inhaled, but with fast breathing there is *not enough time* to exhale and relax.

Your breath should come from your diaphragm, *not* from your chest.

To figure out if you're breathing correctly, place your fist on your abdomen, just below your last rib - you should feel your stomach expand and see your shoulders rise and fall as you breathe.

Practice your breathing by inhaling deeply, allowing the air to fill your belly.

Breathe in for a count of five seconds... then exhale for another five.

Get used to this method of breathing, then try to work it into your everyday speech.

Remember that sitting or standing up straight, with your chin up and your shoulders back, will help you to breathe deeper and project your voice more easily.

It will also give you an air of confidence as you speak.

Try to breathe at the end of every sentence... if you use the deep breathing method, you should have enough air to get through the next sentence without having to pause for breath.

This will also give your listeners a chance to absorb what you're saying.

Good breathing is essential for two reasons:

1. BY USING FULL LUNG CAPACITY, THE BREATH WILL SUPPORT the voice and the voice will become richer, fuller and stronger.

This will *benefit* individuals who have a *small voice* and who worry they cannot be heard when speaking to a group of people.

Volume is controlled in the abdomen not in the throat, so breathing to full strength will allow for greater control of the voice.

2. Breathing deeply and rhythmically has a calming and therapeutic effect as it releases tension and promotes relaxation.

People who are relaxed are more balanced, receptive and confident.

It is no coincidence that many religions use rhythmic breathing techniques such as meditation, yoga and silent contemplation, and vocal release in the form of chants, mantras or hymn singing as aids to their devotions.

By easing physical tension, mental stress decreases and the mind is effectively freed to follow creative pursuits.

Here is another Breathing Exercise for you to practice.

Stand in an easy position with your feet one pace apart, with your knees 'unlocked' and not rigidly pushed back.

Keep your spine straight, your head balanced and face muscles relaxed.

Breathe in... to a slow count of three, then out... to a slow count of three.

Try not to raise your shoulders as you breathe.

Breathe *in* through your nose and *out* through your mouth.

Consciously think of your breath 'filling down' to the bottom of your lungs.

Put the palm of your hand flat against your abdomen and feel the movement.

Push slightly against your hand as you breathe in and out.

Repeat this exercise ten times.

Depending on how you feel after several days of doing this exercise, extend the count of the out-going breath from three to four, five and six gradually building up to ten before you need to take another breath.

Then count out loud on the out-going breath from one to ten. Repeat five times.

By building up your control of *out-going breath*, you will never sound 'breathy' or feel you are 'running out of breath' when you speak to a group or a meeting.

HERE'S ANOTHER BREATHING EXERCISE: PRACTICE READING aloud.

In order to work on *pronunciation, pace and volume*, it's a good idea to *practice* reading aloud.

Pick a passage from a book or magazine, or better yet, find a transcript of a famous speech (such as one by Dr. Martin Luther King Jr.) and read it aloud to yourself.

Remember to stand up straight, breathe deeply and open your mouth fully when you speak.

Stand in front of a mirror if it helps.

Keep practicing until you are happy with what you hear.

Then try to employ the same techniques as part of your everyday speech.

Another helpful strategy to develop your voice is to record yourself.

Even though most people don't like listening to the sound of their own voices, it's a good idea to record yourself speaking.

This can help you to pick up on any faults you wouldn't normally pick up on, such as *mispronunciations* and *speed* or *pitch* problems.

You don't need a recording studio or expensive equipment to record your voice.

Nowadays, most 'smart' phones will have a recording app that you can use to listen to yourself. Or there are inexpensive digital recorders you can use.

You could also use a video camera (which could be helpful to check your posture, eye contact and mouth movement).

Most of us are not used to hearing our own voices and these feelings are totally normal.

Get past the initial, 'Do I really sound like that?' stage and develop a better understanding of your voice.

When relaxed... you will feel more confident, therefore by listening to your voice at home you will have an idea of how you sound to other people.

Although you can't hear your voice in the same way that others hear you, you can develop an awareness of its impact on others. Understanding the physical nature of your voice will give you more control over the way that you use it.

Individuals are used to using language in an informal way in their everyday lives, but as soon as a hint of *formality* is suggested, they can become self-conscious and seize up.

This becomes especially obvious when speaking in front of strangers in a public setting.

The more you get used to the sound of your voice functioning in a slightly more formal way, the easier it is when doing it 'for real'.

In *conversational mode*, individuals *tend* to speak in short phrases, a few at a time.

Reading aloud helps you to become used to the more *fluent* sound of your voice.

Smile as you speak.

A good way to make your tone more friendly and warm is to smile while you speak.

Smiling can help you seem more confident, believable and open to your audience.

People will judge you and the content of your speech more favorably if you use an open, friendly, encouraging tone (as opposed to an aggressive, sarcastic or bored one).

Not a crazed grin, mind you, but even a slight upturn of the corners of your mouth can make the sound of your voice more appealing - even over the phone.

Of course, smiling isn't always appropriate, especially if you're discussing a serious issue.

But remember that inserting emotion into your voice (whatever emotion it may be) can do wonders.

IN THE NEXT LESSON WE LOOK AT **HOW GESTURES CAN ADD** to your oral presentations.

Three things matter in a speech: Who says it, how it's said and what is said and of the three, the last matters the least. John Morley

    If in doubt, leave it out. George Bernard Shaw

"Effective communication is 20% what you know and 80% how you feel about what you know." Jim Rohn

---

CHAPTER ELEVEN: USING GESTURES FOR A POWERFUL SPEECH

I n this chapter, we look closely at **using gestures to add power** to your speech to add life to your oral presentations.

WE START OFF WITH AN OVERVIEW OF GESTURES.

Adding gestures to your presentation can kick your *effectiveness* as a speaker up a notch.

Gestures are specific body movements that reinforce a verbal message.

When you use body movements and gestures appropriately, your presentation takes on a certain sense of *aliveness* that is often hard to accomplish when you use words alone.

Gestures include your posture, the movement of your eyes, hands, face, arms and head, as well as your entire body.

They help to support or reinforce a particular thought or emotion.

If our gestures support our statements, we are communicating with a second sense. People tend to understand and remember messages better when more than one sense is reached.

Winston Churchill was a master at using gestures to powerfully bring home his point.

During World War II, Churchill rallied the citizens of Great Britain to continue their fight against overwhelming odds.

He often visited the neighborhoods of London, which had been devastated by bombs and walked through them with his fingers held up in the sign of a "V".

This victory sign accompanied his famous message, *"Never give in. Never, never, never... give in."*

This gesture so powerfully communicated Churchill's message that soon people gained greater resolve to continue fighting whenever they saw the victory sign.

A speaker's gestures can suggest very precise bits of meaning to an audience.

To be effective, a speaker's gestures must be purposeful.

They must also have the same meaning to the audience as they do to the speaker.

Gestures reflect *not only what is being said*, but the *personality* behind the message.

Gestures **clarify and support** your words - they strengthen the audience's understanding of your verbal message.

Gestures ***dramatize*** your ideas - they help paint **vivid** pictures in your listener's minds.

Gestures lend *emphasis and vitality* - they **underscore** your feelings and attitudes.

Gestures help dissipate nervous tension - they are a **good** outlet for nervous energy.

Gestures function as visual aids - they **enhance** audience attentiveness and retention.

Gestures **stimulate** audience participation - they help elicit the response you want.

It has been said that over **55%** of our body language is communicated to others very clearly.

Another reason using appropriate gestures is so critical to your presentation is communication doesn't just consist of words.

On the other hand, less than **10%** of the words we use in speaking gets through to others.

Whether you're trying to sell your product or service to a client... or you're trying to persuade a group of people to change their behavior, it's **critical** that your words and gestures match.

Many people have sabotaged their messages because their words were saying one thing, while their bodies were saying the exact opposite.

Can you think of a time when someone told you that he would be able to do something while his head was shaking no? Which did you believe, the words or his gesture?

When your body movements are congruent with your words, your message will have a very powerful impact on your audience.

Let's look at gestures even closer.

Gestures are grouped into four categories:

1. Descriptive Gestures. These are used to *clarify or enhance* your message.

Some descriptive gestures include using your hands to indicate size, weight, shape, direction or location, and the function of something.

Comparison and contrast can be illustrated by moving your hands in unison to show similarities and by *moving them* in opposite directions to show differences.

2. Emphatic Gestures. These gestures underscore or add impact to what is being said. Show your audience how *important* your point is.

For example, a clenched fist suggests strong feelings such as anger or determination. It can also indicate power.

Hitting your fist into your open palm could illustrate anger or importance.

A forefinger pointing toward the ceiling means that people should listen to what you are saying.

Folding your arms across your chest projects strength and determination.

Clasping your hands in front of your chest conveys unity, a good gesture to use when you are emphasizing team work or trying to resolve a conflict.

3. SUGGESTIVE GESTURES. THESE ARE SYMBOLS OF IDEAS OR emotions.

For example, an open palm suggests giving or receiving, while a shrug of the shoulders indicates ignorance, perplexity, or irony.

4. Prompting Gestures. These are used to evoke a desired response from the audience.

For example, if you want your listeners to raise their hand, applaud, or perform some other action, you will encourage the desired response by doing the act yourself as an example.

Let's look at the Location of Gestures.

Gestures can help you paint pictures with words, but make sure they don't get in the way.

You can make gestures above, below, or at or near your shoulders; each position produces a different effect on your speech delivery.

1. Gestures *above the shoulders* suggest physical height, inspiration, or emotion.
2. Gestures *below the shoulders* indicate sadness, rejection, apathy, or condemnation.
3. Gestures *at or near the shoulders* suggest calmness or serenity.

The most frequently used gesture involves an open palm held outward toward the audience.

Holding your palm *outward* implies giving or receiving.

Unfortunately, most speakers use this gesture unconsciously as a general movement without any specific meaning.

A palm *held downward* expresses suppression, secrecy, completion, or stability.

A PALM *HELD UPWARD* AND OUTWARD SUGGESTS STOPPING.

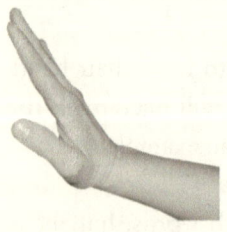

HANDS ALSO IMPLY *MEASUREMENT* SUCH AS TALL, SHORT, SMALL, long, and so on.

Make the Most Out of Your Movement

Caution: Movement ought to be *motivated* by the content of your speech.

Sometimes, speakers wander without apparent aim, creating a distraction with too much movement or too many gestures.

As you practice your speech, experiment with different gestures to find those that feel natural to you and underscore your message.

People will begin to make judgments about you as soon as you stand up.

The time to begin using effective body movements is when you walk to your position in front of a group.

Stand up tall and walk with a strong posture.

Let your *body* communicate you have something important to say and the audience needs to hear it.

If your posture is slouched, they will feel you aren't convinced about your message and they will begin doubting you before you have uttered a single word.

When you get to the front, take a deep breath, calmly look at your entire audience and smile.

One of the biggest mistakes presenters make is to begin talking as soon as they get up to the front, or even worse, as they are walking there.

When you take time to look at your audience before you speak, you begin to establish a critical connection with them.

You also give the audience sufficient time to focus on you and what you are about to say.

It is important to look directly at the faces of your audience members, not over their heads.

Eye contact is one of the most important aspects of speaking.

An easy way to get over stage fright is to look at the faces of individual audience members and just talk to that one person *instead* of the entire audience.

Rotate the people you talk to—someone on the left, someone

towards the middle, a person on the right, someone in the front, etc.

This will help you maintain rapport with the entire group, while allowing you to feel at ease.

A further advantage of maintaining good eye contact is it will help you gauge how your message is coming across to the group.

If you are trying to explain something and members of the audience, give you blank stares, then you need to adjust your words so they can better understand you.

Let's look at some Simple Tips to Using Gestures

1. Keep the gestures above the waist. Low hand gestures are hard to see and may indicate low self-esteem in the person using them.

2. Use gestures to reinforce a point. But be careful. It's not that uncommon to accidentally confuse your audience with your gestures e.g., making two key points, but holding up three fingers.

3. Avoid jerky gestures. The normal gestures you would use in conversation may be too quick to use in front of an audience of more than one person. They may make you appear nervous or jumpy.

When presenting to a group, hold your gestures longer than you would in normal conversation.

4. Vary your gestures. If you're right-handed, resist the urge to gesture only with your right hand. Switch from hand to hand and occasionally use both hands at once. If you use the same gesture over and over again, it loses its impact.

Now we'll look at using Conversational Gestures.

Like Winston Churchill, you should strive to incorporate gestures into your talk.

People naturally use gestures in conversations.

They are not on the spot, so they easily move their arms and hands and make facial expressions to illustrate the points they are trying to make.

However, an amazing thing happens when people stand up in front of a group to speak.

They suddenly think, "Oh no! What am I going to do with these things attached to my shoulders?" and they either don't move them at all or they move them awkwardly.

Gestures should be a natural extension of who we are.

Presenters should strive to be themselves.

They should be as spontaneous with their movements as if they were talking to their family or friends.

Practice Makes Natural:

A good way to be comfortable with gestures is to know your speech well.

Several of the most outstanding speakers offer the same piece of advice: "The key to effectively using gestures is to know your material so well, to be so well prepared, that your gestures will flow naturally."

Practice your speech and know it well so that you can enjoy sharing your message with others.

Become a master at using your body to support your words.

Have fun with gestures, be yourself, and you will certainly present your message with power and pizzazz.

IN THE NEXT CHAPTER WE LOOK AT SOME ADVICE FROM Toastmasters International on **using your voice and your image** to add life to your oral presentations.

As human beings we need to communicate with others so that we may reveal ourselves and identify with others. This urge to communicate, the awareness of being an entity, helps us to secure real contact with the world about us and find acceptance and understanding. Dominick A. Barbara

"Good communication is as stimulating as black coffee, and just as hard to sleep after." Anne Morrow Lindberg, American Author

Words have the power to destroy or heal. When words are true and kind they can change the world. Buddha

CHAPTER TWELVE: YOUR VOICE AND YOUR IMAGE

Toastmasters International publishes an excellent booklet entitled 'Your Speaking Voice.'

HERE IS A BRIEF SECTION FROM THE BOOKLET THAT I WANT TO share.

Your voice and your face are your public relations agents.

More than any other factor, they serve to establish an image of you in the minds of others.

Your face, body, and speech are the interpreters of your mind.

They reveal your character—the real you—as nothing else can.

A smile—whether it starts in your face, your disposition, or your voice – reacts on the other elements and tends to induce a positive, constructive complex which makes your attitude and appearance attractive and pleasing.

Your best voice can help bring out your best self.

Nature has given you a priceless gift in your voice.

It is the means by which you can communicate with others—the medium of your message.

It also makes possible understanding and camaraderie. Take advantage of the information and exercises in this booklet, because by your voice and your words, you influence others.

Then, there are an infinite number of ways in which you can use your pitch, rate, volume and quality to add additional interest and variety when the need arises.

Enjoy the process.

༺༻

"You cannot speak that which you do not know. You cannot share that which you do not feel. You cannot translate that which you do not have. And you cannot give that which you do not possess. To give it and to share it, and for it to be effective, you first need to have it. Good communication starts with good preparation." Jim Rohn

First learn the meaning of what you say, and then speak. Epictetus (55-135)

"The goal of effective communication should be for listeners to say, 'Me, too!' verses 'So what?' Jim Rohn

❦ II ❧
PART II: ADDITIONAL RESOURCES

This section contains questions about public speaking that were answered by the author on Quora.com.

ARE STOPS AND PAUSES NECESSARY WHILE PUBLIC SPEAKING?

No, I don't believe stops and pauses are necessary while public speaking however, if you want to become an effective public speaker and improve your messages there is value in adding pauses.

I've seen many speakers who are fast talkers and their presentation is like a road race, they are fighting to get it over as fast as they can. I usually find myself saying "breathe, breathe."

I believe there is value in adding a pause at certain points in your presentation to allow your audience to consider the point you made before you move on to your next thought.

It has been suggested you pause every 5 or 6 words to allow your audience to think about what you're saying before you move on to your next thought. This may be appropriate in a presentation where the details are crucial and you need to give your audience time to process each point before introducing a new one. I think this would create a boring presentation and I would probably walk out on it.

Your presentation needs to have a balance of pace: example, parts of your presentation should be rapid to share something exciting, it should be slowed down at times where your content is somber. It should have variations in volume and pitch as well.

I recall a presentation I delivered at a Toastmasters meeting. It was a serious topic I was speaking about, and at a certain point I had forgotten my next line. I paused for a few seconds to think of the line. My speech evaluator advised me my pause was perfectly placed and was the best part of my presentation. From then on, I tried to incorporate dramatic pauses in strategic places within my presentations.

WHEN YOU GIVE A PRESENTATION, DO YOU STICK TO A SCRIPT OR DO YOU REACT AT THE MOMENT?

It depends.
 It depends on the type of presentation you're delivering and the purpose of the presentation.
For example, if you're delivering a canned sales pitch, that is one where you have a pre-written script with the expectation you follow it word for word, and questions arose, you may want to defer to the end of your presentation to answer those questions.
Similarly, if you're delivering a presentation that contained a lot of data or information, you may want to deliver your presentation without any interruptions.
Conversely, if you were delivering an educational style of presentation where you wanted your audience to keep up with you, you may welcome and answer questions before moving on to new content.
As a presenter, I utilize both techniques i.e. I may answer questions on the spot, or I may defer them to later time. As you become more comfortable in presenting, it becomes easier to answer questions on the fly. The challenge is in deciding whether to answer the question if said question adds to an understanding of the content you're delivering at this point in time or deter-

mining if it could it take you off in a different direction you don't want to go?

One technique that helps deal with questions that are off-topic is to use a parking lot. The parking lot could be a section of the whiteboard or perhaps a flip chart. The idea is questions that are off-topic rather than ignoring them, they are added to the parking lot and then at the end of your session you should deal with them at that time.

WHY IS PUBLIC SPEAKING A PERFORMANCE?

To answer this question in the affirmative, I would have to agree with the statement public speaking is a performance, however I don't.

The term performance to me indicates there is an element of acting to the speech delivery.

I'm not saying that performing is a bad thing, in fact I believe many speech presentations can benefit from adding theatrics to the delivery of the content.

However, not all presentations are appropriate for theatrics or performing as the original question would indicate.

For example, my understanding of the American verses the Canadian legal systems. The theatrics we see on television with American lawyers performing in the courtroom would never be tolerated in a Canadian courtroom.

It is often recommended that every presentation can benefit from adding humor. Even a eulogy or celebration of life can benefit from the injection of humor. It may not go over so well though if the eulogy deliverer went into theatrical mode. It may be attention grabbing, but would it really be appropriate given the setting?

Adding characters to your presentation with different vocalizations to identify those characters to the audience can be beneficial for delivering your message. Having your characters say something positive about you can go a long way in building your credibility. If you say something about yourself, it may be considered bragging. However, if your characters say something about you, it can be considered a testimonial.

While I don't agree with the original statement that public speaking is a performance, I will say that adding theatrics to certain types of presentations can be beneficial.

AS A SPEAKER, HOW DO YOU MAKE YOUR PRESENTATION APPEAR EFFORTLESS?

While some of my speeches may seem effortless to new speakers, there really is a lot of effort put into the presentation behind-the-scenes.

The most obvious factor you'd expect to hear to make your presentation appear effortless would be to practice, practice, and practice more.

While that is good advice, you need to go back even further to the speech development phase. Your presentation needs to be crafted in a way that it attracts and holds your audience's attention.

Then looking at the flow of the logistics of your presentation you need to ask yourself whether there are any awkward parts or are there difficult areas for you to deliver or even to remember the content.

While you may have practiced your presentation numerous times, are you passionate about your topic?

If you're creating a presentation, you will be using over and over again in different settings, it becomes easier to analyze your presentation to see what worked and what didn't work. You can then adjust your presentation for the next time.

When you are delivering a presentation on only one occasion, it can be a lot more challenging making your presentation seem effortless.

So how do we make our presentation seem effortless? There is an old adage I like to use:

"How do you eat an elephant?" Answer "one bite at a time."

Instead of trying to focus on making the entire presentation as a single entity effortless, break your presentation down into individual chunks.

Take each chunk, focus on it, analyze it for effectiveness i.e. does it add to your presentation, did your message come across?

Then take each chunk and practice it. Don't memorize your speech linearly. Learn the content of each chunk inside out. Note that I said *learn* not *memorize*. The problem with memorizing your speech word for word linearly, is if something happens during your presentation or interferes with your concentration, it can be difficult to get back on track.

When you have learned the content using the chunk method you will have likely learned more material than you can deliver at that occasion. This can be advantageous if you have been given less time to deliver your presentation, or even more for that matter, you can effortlessly adapt the time for your presentation.

The effortlessness comes into play when you are thoroughly prepared to deliver your presentation no matter what obstacles are placed in your way.

Don't forget to have fun!

HOW SHOULD YOU REHEARSE GIVING A SPEECH IN FRONT OF A MIRROR VS IN FRONT OF A VIDEO CAMERA?

I would suggest you don't use either technique for practicing your speech.

Let's start off with the problem of using a mirror. It is an artificial situation. In essence, it is a mirror reflection of what you are doing at a given point in time... reflection being the key word.

When you're speaking to a mirror and you're watching yourself and your gestures, it is difficult to stay focused on the words you plan to speak and the gestures you plan on using.

Practicing in front of the video camera has a better chance of providing you a different perspective, i.e. one from the audience as to how your presentation went.

The problem is for many new speakers when they view the video they tend to focus on their perceived weaknesses. To improve your public speaking skills, you need to maximize the speaking skills you already have, not dwelling on the weaknesses you perceive.

An alternative to using video or talking to a mirror is to use a digital voice recorder. The value of using this digital voice recorder is you can focus on the content of your speech. Delivering your speech several times and having a digital record gives you the opportunity to replay the presentation which in turn helps you memorize your presentation.

Another advantage using a digital audio recording is that you can test out different versions of a sentence or paragraph you want to deliver. Sometimes when you write a speech the copy that is the text may look okay in writing but when you actually deliver it orally, it can be a tongue twister, or perhaps not even make sense.

After you have recorded an audio version of your presentation a few times, then I would suggest you try recording yourself on video. However, I would add that when you record your video that you have actual people in your audience to speak to. Otherwise speaking to a video camera may turn out to be just as stilted as it would've been if you're speaking to your mirror.

IS IT EASY TO MAKE AN INFORMATIVE SPEECH? WHY? WHY NOT?

'Easy' is a relative term. What I consider being easy may be considered impossible for another.

There are several elements involved in making an informative speech.

Firstly, you need to have the skills to be able to research your topic. To inform somebody else, you need to be knowledgeable about the subject yourself.

Secondly, you need to be able to filter the content so you deliver the right amount for the time you have and the understanding level of your audience. We are in the information age. There will always be too much information available for any topic.

And thirdly, you need to have the communication and public speaking skills to get your message across effectively.

Other factors come into play such as the topic. A light-hearted topic may be easy to deliver. Whereas a topic such as a public or personal tragedy, may be very difficult to speak about, even if you have good public speaking skills.

WHERE SHOULD I LOOK IF I AM GIVING A SPEECH TO AN AUDIENCE?

I don't claim to be an expert, however, with 25 years of Toastmasters speaking opportunities, I am experienced and feel comfortable in providing an answer.

The simplest and perhaps most precise answer to the question of where should I look... would be to look at the audience.

So, what does that mean? I don't like giving speeches. However, I do like having conversations with groups of people. I tend to think of a speech as a one-way data dump. You are often pressured to get your message out at the expense of your audience.

When you think of having a conversation with your audience, as I am suggesting, you are open to interaction with them. This interaction can be elicited by asking rhetorical or even direct questions to them.

It is easier to make eye contact when conversing versus preaching. Many speeches are preachy. That one -way data dump I referred to earlier.

A technique I had heard that helps reduce your reluctance to maintain eye contact with your audience is to greet people at the entrance, when they come in to sit down. That way, when you are speaking to them in your presentation, you are speaking to them as friends, not strangers. I have found it helpful and I can tend to be on the shy side. One caveat is that you want to protect your voice when you are greeting people, so it will serve you well when you do speak.

The beauty of making eye contact with your audience is that many of your audience members will feel that you are speaking to them directly. Connecting with every audience member should be your objective. Otherwise, why bother speaking at all?

HOW CAN I LEARN TO ENJOY PUBLIC SPEAKING?

I'm going to play Devil's advocate somewhat by starting with I don't believe you can learn to enjoy anything in life. You either enjoy something or you don't.

I don't care for fiery hot sauces. I can't imagine learning to enjoy them.

Maybe the question you are really asking is 'how can I enjoy public speaking' or 'how can I be a public speaker without being afraid or nervous?'

Having been a Toastmaster going on 25 years I do a lot of public speaking. I enjoy public speaking most of the time because I'm speaking about something, I am knowledgeable or passionate about. And I've learned I love an audience.

Sometimes I need to speak on a matter that is controversial or contentious. I don't enjoy those situations.

Darren Lacroix was the Toastmasters World Champion of Speaking in 2001. He says the secret to becoming a better public speaker is 'stage time... stage time... stage time.'

Practice makes perfect. To enjoy public speaking, you need to be skilled at speaking in various situations. In time, you will develop your self-confidence and begin to seek out speaking opportunities that will challenge you. Also, in time, people will be seeking you out to offer you speaking opportunities.

Go for it! Enjoy yourself.

ABOUT THE AUTHOR

Rae A. Stonehouse is a Canadian born author & speaker. His professional career as a Registered Nurse working predominantly in psychiatry/mental health, has spanned four decades.

Rae has embraced the principal of CANI (Constant and Never-ending Improvement) as promoted by thought leaders such as Tony Robbins and brings that philosophy to each of his publications and presentations.

Rae has dedicated the latter segment of his journey through life to overcoming his personal inhibitions. As a 25+ year member of Toastmasters International he has systematically built his self-confidence and communicating ability. He is passionate about sharing his lessons with his readers and listeners.

His publications thus far are of the self-help, self-improvement genre and systematically offer valuable sage advice on a specific topic.

His writing style can be described as being conversational. As an author, Rae strives to have a one-to-one conversation with each of his readers, very much like having your own personal self-development coach.

Rae is known for having a wry sense of humour that features in his publications. To learn more about Rae A. Stonehouse, visit the Wonderful World of Rae Stonehouse at http://raestonehouse.com.

ALSO BY RAE A. STONEHOUSE

PROtect Yourself! Empowering Tips & Techniques for Personal Safety: A Practical Violence Prevention Manual for Healthcare Workers https://books2read.com/protectyourself

POWER OF PROMOTION: ON-LINE MARKETING FOR Toastmasters Club Growth
https://books2read.com/powerofpromotion

YOU'RE HIRED! JOB SEARCH STRATEGIES THAT WORK (This is the complete program)
E-book & Paperback: https://books2read.com/yourehired
On-line E-course: (Available as a self-directed or instructor-led program) http://liveforexcellenceacademy.com/

You're Hired! Resume Tactics: Job Search Strategies That Work
E-book & Paperback: https://books2read.com/resumetactics
On-line E-course: http://liveforexcellenceacademy.com/

❦

Job Interview Preparation: Job Search Strategies That Work
E-book & Paperback: https://books2read.com/jobinterviewpreparation
On-line E-course: http://liveforexcellenceacademy.com/

❦

You're Hired! Leveraging Your Network: Job Search Strategies That Work
E-book & Paperback: https://books2read.com/leveragingyournetwork
On-line E-course: http://liveforexcellenceacademy.com/

❦

You're Hired! Power Tactics: Job Search Strategies That Work (This is a box set containing the complete content of Resume Tactics, Job Interview Preparation & Leveraging Your Network)
E-book: https://books2read.com/powertactics

❦

Power Networking for Shy People: How to Network Like a Pro

E-book & **Paperback:** https://books2read.com/networklikeapronetworklikeapro

❧

The Savvy Emcee: How to be a Dynamic Master of Ceremonies
 E-book: The Savvy Emcee: How to be a Dynamic Master of Ceremonies E-book
 Working With Words: How to Add Life to Your Oral Presentations is also available as an on-line course at https://liveforexcellenceacademy.com

If you have found this book and program to be helpful, please leave us a warm review wherever you purchased this book.

www.ingramcontent.com/pod-product-compliance
Lightning Source LLC
Chambersburg PA
CBHW020546080526
44583CB00013B/1012